Page One

Coming in second now...

EMPTY

By

Ed Chandler

Three times

Where has the copyright gone?

Will you find it?

Try lucky number seven...

Four I think...

An Empty Fifth

Over the next page are
The rights of this book

Solitary Six

THE
SEVENTH PAGE

8

Each page number is marked differently,
But each page is still marked...

All this book is and shall ever be is....

EMPTY....

With no introduction the book seamlessly
began...

But where was it?

Nine

What was it?

When was it?

How was it even a book?

Sometimes in life we never get the answers to all the questions we have...

For life is often...

EMPTY

But then again...

It was never...

What you expected...

And now the book turned sideways...

(Turn book on its side to read next part)

Eleven

On the side-line of words...
In desperate times...
And on the left this time...

XII

After this and that...

The book went on...

EMPTY

Having found normality....

Having got rid of it....

Having a good time?

For all this book was...

Thirteen

For all this book is...

EMPTY

Something else happened...

Something else occurred...

There was more than one event,

But never more than two...

For the book still remained unfulfilled

14

Completely...

EMPTY

And turning on its side once more....

(Turn book the other way now...)

Fifteen

Over on the right
Flipped it and reflected it...

And that was that...

Or was it....

As for no reason what so ever now...

Having turned the book

This way

And that way

       The whole thing suddenly

       And without this warning

       It turned upside down!

         Seventeen

Something from down under...
Something under hand...
The book was turned over...
It was more backwards...
Than forwards...
And for now we go back to normal...

18

Now this might not be upside down, so sorry...
I wanted it to be upside down, but wasn't allowed.

Back to reality....

But still

EMPTY

The story was here, but

There

Were

No

Words

Well hardly any at all....

Not even a thousand, if you count them....

Nineteen

Oh look...

The
    Words
        Are
            Falling
                Off
                    The
                        Page...
                            Well
                                Almost...
                                    Any
                                     W
                                     A
                                     Y

BANG!

And then with that....

The book was over....

Well no it wasn't

For you have to go to the back now....

Go backwards in order to come forwards....

The book goes upside down

And then back to front, sort of...

Have fun!

And if it doesn't quite work then, I apologise...

The End

========================

Well as the words pour out...
As the closing elements gather...
The final...
As we reach...
The End,
It was all over...
22

This is supposed to be upside down...

Vacant a little
Clear and without...
Many words...
But it was all here...
I think...
Twenty-three

Again this should be upside down...

Now this book
It was short....
Bare...
But not the animal...
More blank or just EMPTY...
24

Should also be upside down...

All of a sudden you found me...
Well done for that....
Well done for buying this....
Empty Book
25

This was the last page (first) to be upside down and
then you'd work your way backwards.

Just before you flip me over

And go backwards,

I would like to say

Thank you....

Twenty-six

www.ingramcontent.com/pod-product-compliance
Lightning Source LLC
LaVergne TN
LVHW020101190726
843498LV00012B/1922

9 786599 409387